Good People Go to Hell, Bad People Go to Heaven

FR. BERNARD CHAMPAGNE

AND

JAY MCCURTTEN

PAGE PUBLISHING, INC.
New York, NY

First originally published by Page Publishing, Inc. 2018

ISBN 978-1-64138-645-6 (Paperback)
ISBN 978-1-64138-646-3 (Digital)

Printed in the United States of America

Meditate Daily On

Death

Judgment

Heaven

and

Hell

All Bible verses taken from the Douay Rheims Bible.

soulsavinginfo.com

Preface

You may have read the title of this book and decided to read it out of sheer curiosity, or perhaps you're looking to find out as much information as you can in the hopes of ensuring your spot in Heaven. Our goal with this book is to get you, the reader, to have a proper understanding of some of the things that are required to earn eternal salvation. While not everyone will agree with the contents and message of this book, it is based on strict and historic Christian teachings.

There will be many who are not familiar with the information presented in this book. With the embrace of modernism in the church today, these teachings seem to have been lost to a more worldlier way of thinking. You must understand that for two thousand years, these were the teachings of the Church.

You may at times feel that this book is lecturing you or being harsh and accusatory. The goal of this book is not to insult anyone but merely have you take an honest look at how you're living your spiritual life. Nobody wants to be told what to do, and we certainly don't want to be told that what we are doing may be wrong or insufficient. When this happens, we usually feel insulted or even angry. This book may have the potential of doing that, but this only happens when we're forced to take a truthful look at ourselves.

The teachings in this book come from the extensive experience of Father Bernard Champagne. Father Bernard started his journey of learning the Christian faith in the fourth grade when his teacher, Sister Concetta, was unable to answer his question "If the Catholic Church is the one true church, why are there Protestants?" Her response, "Don't ask foolish questions" angered him and lit the fire for him knowing the truth not only about the Catholic religion but all other religions as well. From that day on, he chose to spend his time at the library, immersed in reading instead of the usual activities children participate in.

After high school, he joined the Trappist religious order where he spent the next sixteen years cloistered from the world in a monastery. Those years were spent in daily lessons of Christian teachings, church history, theology, philosophy, and learning about the fathers of the church and the great saints, among many other teachings. In 1967, as the church was beginning to take on changes and embrace modernism, he chose to leave the Trappist order and joined the Benedictines, who, at that point, still observed a stricter way of life. Four years later, as the Benedictines began to embrace the church's newfound modernism, he left their monastery as well. In 1977, he was ordained a priest. The next twenty years took him to various parts of the U.S. and Canada, celebrating Mass and preaching. In 2002, he settled in Orange, Connecticut, where he resides as the pastor of Our Lady of Sorrows Church. His pursuit of educating himself on the Christian faith has never stopped, and you can usually find him sitting at his kitchen table with a book in his hands. To say he has a vast understanding of Christian teachings would be an understatement.

Neither Father Bernard nor myself have ever written anything professional before. To the experienced reader, you may find this book to be unpolished. We wanted to write it in the spirit of how it happened— two people sitting around, having a conversation about their eternal destiny and what's required of it. Perhaps after reading this book, you may sit back and reflect on what it offers.

This book is a simple first step to learning the things we all must do in the hopes of earning eternal salvation. We hope you'll benefit from the teachings it provides.

Introduction

It's finally beginning to feel like spring. I noticed, as we walked out of church after Mass, that the last of the snow had finally melted and you can see the trees forming the tiniest of buds. After the winter that just wouldn't end here in New England, it's a very welcome sight. Stopping to look back at the few but faithful parishioners exiting our small white church that has stood the test of time (having been built in 1835), I'm still pondering one of the most intriguing statements I've ever heard in my life. During Father Bernard's sermon this week, he made an amazing revelation, "Good people go to hell and bad people go to Heaven." What? Are you completely insane? I'm thinking to myself, trying to keep in mind that he is now eighty-one years old and while the most knowledgeable person I've ever known on God and religion, I'm wondering, after hearing this statement, if he's beginning to lose it. I can't wait for everybody to leave so I can get him in the kitchen of the rectory to ask him about this profound statement.

Suddenly, I hear his old voice cry out, "Jay, unlock the door, please." Adjacent to the church is the rectory. It's a small one-story building only about sixty feet long, two-thirds of which is a small chapel and sitting area with a beautiful old stone fireplace and the rest is Father Bernard's personal living area. He has two long-haired cats, one is twenty years old and the other is eight years old; the younger one is full of playfulness, while the older one just wants to sleep.

Father Bernard says the traditional Latin Mass. I am one of his altar servers, and in addition to the basic duties of a server, I'm also a lector. Except for the gospel and his sermon, he says the Mass entirely in Latin. To engage the parishioners more deeply in the Mass, I also translate the prayers into English while he says them simultaneously in Latin. In 1948, Pope Pius XII requested all the bishops of the world to introduce this dialog Mass and Father Bernard upholds this tradition.

We chitchat with some of the parishioners for a few minutes, and finally, everyone leaves. We go into the kitchen, and as usual, Father makes a beeline for the coffee pot. He pours himself a cup and puts in his light cream. I'm a tea drinker, so I begin to boil some water for myself. We sit down at the kitchen table and I'm staring at him, still trying to wrap my head around this bizarre statement he let loose during his sermon. So far, there's been complete silence.

Our Lady of Sorrows Sanctuary

Chapter 1

"What the heck was that?"

"Why are you staring at me?" Father asks.

"What the heck was that?" I retort.

"What was what?"

"That thing you said in your sermon."

"I said a lot of things in my sermon."

"You know, 'good people go to Hell, and bad people go to Heaven.'"

"Yeah, what about it? It's true!" he says.

"What do you mean, it's true?"

"Well, it is."

"How can you say that?" I ask.

"What do you mean, how can I say that? What should I do, lie to everybody?"

"No, you shouldn't lie, but it doesn't make any sense. How are good people going to Hell, and bad people going to Heaven?"

"It makes perfect sense if you know God, but how many people know God? Do they even want to know Him?" Father says.

"I don't know. They're here. They must want to know Him," I respond.

He lets out a loud "Ha! Believe me, most people don't want to know God. If they did, they would live their lives much differently."

"How much differently do you want them to live? They're coming to church every week, trying to obey God's laws, what else do you want from them?" I ask.

"My God, are you serious? How many people go to church because they love God?" he asks. "Very few, trust me. The average churchgoer attends Mass out of obligation or it's their routine, not because they love God. That's why the saints have taught us the fewness of the saved. What did the Blessed Virgin say at Fatima? 'Souls are falling daily into Hell like snowflakes.' Think about that! They're not all bad people. They're not all murderers, rapists, and robbers. They're average, everyday good people who are in love with the world, not God."

"Alright, wait a minute. So you're saying that being a good person, obeying the rules of society, being (hopefully) a good husband, wife, parent, or friend, earning a decent, honest living, having a good heart, and trying to help others whenever possible can put you in Hell?" I ask.

"Absolutely!" he responds.

"What are you talking about?" I ask.

"Listen, while all of those things are very good, and of course, we should all strive to live that way, where is God in all of that? On Sunday for an hour? I hate to rain on your spiritual parade but it takes more than that to be saved. Those are worldly goals. You can't develop a relationship with Christ by spending one hour a week with Him. It takes daily effort on our part to build a relationship with Christ. And without that relationship, you'll never fall in love with Christ. And if you don't love Christ above all things, then what hope is there for your soul? Let me ask you a question that you and every Catholic should know, why are we here?" Father asks.

"Easy enough. To know, love and serve God," I respond.

"Correct!" He exclaims. "In the sixth century, the great St. Benedict, who founded communal monastic life, recognized what it would take to develop a personal, intimate relationship with Christ. He taught that you could achieve this relationship by receiving frequent, if not daily, Holy Communion, practicing mental prayer, and doing spiritual reading.

"Now, how many people care about receiving Holy Communion daily? It's very few, I can assure you. As a matter of fact, the thought probably doesn't even enter most people's minds, especially today! It's a completely foreign concept to them, yet it's exactly what our Lord wants from us.

"Mental prayer is so important to the soul. If more people spent time talking to God instead of paying attention to the world every second of their day, they would find themselves being drawn closer to our Lord.

"Take spiritual reading. Most people don't read about God. You'll find useless romance novels and murder mysteries in people's homes, but how many people sit and read about the lives of the saints who've paved the way for our spiritual journey through this world? Few people want to learn about God. They want to watch their reality TV programs, which bring them a moment of brief, transitory pleasure, but you can be sure that they won't get you any closer to salvation.

"To think that people go to church every week out of love for God is very ignorant thinking. Again, most go because it's what they've always done, so they continue to do it. Now, tell this to most people and they'll argue with you. They'll even be angry with you. They want to believe that it's pure love for God that brings them to church every week. But if they were truthful with themselves, they would have to admit otherwise. Anybody can go to Mass. But the truth is, most don't even understand what's going on, and the minute Mass is over, they're out the door and headed right back to the world. They can't even comprehend what they've just experienced. If they did, they would still be in church talking to God.

"They don't because God is not that important in their lives, and it shows by the way most people live they're lives. People live for the world, and if you live for the world, then you love the world. And if you love the world, it is absolutely impossible to love God."

"Why can't you love the world and God?" I ask.

"Because God is not of the world. Remember what Jesus said. 'If the world hates you, know that it has hated me before you. If you were of the world, the world would love what is its own. But because you are not of the world, but I have chosen you out of the world, therefore the world hates you' (John 15:18–19). That's a very powerful statement."

Father continues, "Think of the life Jesus led. It was in poverty, without honor and pride, all the things that this world strives for. To live a life in love with God is to detach yourself from the world in every way and give up all worldly honors. Who's willing to do that? Clearly, most people won't, and they obviously aren't listening to the gospels and sermons being preached.

"Our lord teaches us to be lowly and nothing, to let people walk all over us, and accept it happily for the love of God, but do people do that? No, absolutely not! Their pride is way too great to allow anybody to get the best of them. It goes against everything we, as humans, understand. Unfortunately for most, that pride is the very thing that may end up damning their soul. Not that feeling pride is a sin, but it's the reaction caused by that pride that can put you in a state of mortal sin. When a person is offended by another, they usually react very defensively and try to get the upper hand on the one that's offended them, that would be a sin. But if someone offends you and you don't react with anger but with humility, you will receive tremendous graces from that."

"That's a very difficult way to live your life," I respond.

"Sure, it is. But it's necessary for your spiritual growth. The problem is most people put little or no effort into their spiritual life. Everything I'm sitting here telling you isn't difficult to understand. It's just difficult to do, and why? Because people want to live the way they want to, and no one is going to tell them differently.

"People seem happy being unhappy, and we see it all around us. If you turn on the TV, you will see these reality shows where everybody's angry and fighting with each other. They take something so unimportant and go in front of the world to display their stupidity. Their pride is so important that they're willing to go on national television in the hopes that they might be proven right.

"The hatred and chaos that you see on these shows is exactly what Hell is like. Think about it: constant fighting and hatred, yelling and screaming, never a moment's peace or the feelings of love. That's exactly what souls experience in Hell. Accept that it won't be for one hour like those shows, but for all eternity.

"People have gotten it into their heads that they can live any way they want and there will be no consequences for that way of life. We are all appointed to die, and then comes our judgment before God. What will people say to God for the way they've lived?

"If people would do any spiritual reading, they would realize that simply being a good person is not enough to get you into Heaven."

"Okay, elaborate on that for me, Father," I ask.

"Listen, there is one essential thing necessary to save your soul—love God above all things. Now you're married, you have a daughter, and I know you love them. When you're not with them, how do you feel?"

"I miss them," I respond.

"Right, you desire to be with them," he says.

"With love comes desire. You can't have love without desire. They go hand in hand."

"Yes, of course," I answer.

"So if you truly love Jesus, you will desire to be with Him, and what's the best way to be with Him while here on earth? By receiving Him as often as possible in Holy Communion.

"Now, think about when people are getting ready to go to church each week. Are they so excited that they're going to see Jesus and receive Him in Holy Communion, or does that thought not even enter their minds? You can be assured that most aren't thinking about church that way, and people say they love God, all evidence to the contrary.

"Think about if you couldn't be with your daughter for whatever reason. Your desire to be with her would be so strong that it would be almost unbearable. Why? Because you love her.

"If people truly loved our Lord, they would come by church as often as they could to see Jesus and spend a little time with Him. But the thought of coming by and receiving Jesus outside of Mass is so foreign to people that most wouldn't even consider it. It makes no sense to them, and the reason is because God is not first in their lives. The world is way more important to them than God is. If people don't want to spend their time with Jesus now, why do you think they would want to spend eternity with Him in Heaven?"

"I guess, they wouldn't," I respond.

"Exactly! By the way your waters boiled."

Chapter 2

Frequent Communion

"Do you think people are aware of what you're telling me?" I ask.

"Well, if they did spiritual reading and learned their faith, they would! But most people can't be bothered. They have their own ideas about how to live and what it takes to be saved, and it's very difficult to get most to understand differently. I've been fighting this my whole life—trying to get people to understand beyond their own understanding.

"Let's take daily communion into consideration. St. Benedict, one of the greatest saints of the church, strongly encouraged daily or frequent communion because he knew that it would draw you to a closer relationship with Christ. But do you know how many people aren't even aware of what Holy Communion is?"

"I find that hard to believe, Father."

"No, it's true. I've had people come to me with a problem and ask if I can give them some of that bread I give to other people."

"Some of that bread, seriously?" I respond.

"I'm telling you, I've heard it from people. I then try to explain to them that it's the actual body and blood of Jesus Christ in the Holy Eucharist, but many people can't really comprehend that. Nevertheless, St. Benedict knew that if you were to receive our Lord daily, it will draw you closer to Him. Not only draw you closer to Him, but strengthen you in your daily battles against the devil."

"Daily battles against the devil?" I ask.

"Yes, of course!" he says.

"Every day, we're in a battle against the devil. Most people aren't aware that the struggles they encounter on a daily basis originate from the devil. The devil is constantly at work on us trying to get us to do the wrong thing. It's common to think that it's just part of everyday life but it's not. If people took time to analyze their struggles, they would see very suspicious activity.

"Have you ever wondered why the things you struggle with the most personally are the things that constantly present themselves to you regularly? If you struggle with alcohol, you'll constantly find yourself in a situation where the opportunity to drink is greater. Perhaps you struggle with lust, then everywhere you go, there's going to be that attractive person there to tempt you. These are the works of the devil. He knows your strengths and weaknesses just the way our Lord does, and he uses them to try and make you sin. Nothing is coincidence. It all happens for a reason, and if we're not prepared, we will lose this fight.

"Now I know many people can't make it to daily Mass because of their work schedule, but can't people take a few minutes out of their day to stop by their church and ask to receive Jesus? If people did that, they would have the constant strength to fight off those instances of temptation when they arise. But without the strength of God, we're too weak.

"Going to church and receiving Holy Communion once a week isn't enough ammunition for this fight. Unfortunately, most people don't realize that it's the work of the devil they're up against, and they think they can handle those problems on their own. How many problems in your life have worked out the way you've wanted them to? Also, how much impatience and how much anxiety do you experience when going through these trials? If we realize what strength there is in God, if we're faithful to Him and come to Him often, we would be able to face our problems with such confidence.

"The unfortunate truth is that the average person is extremely prideful, and it's very difficult to admit that you can't handle a problem on your own. Reaching out to somebody, even God makes us feel very uneasy. But isn't that what humility is all about? Very few understand the value and importance of daily Holy Communion. To do this, you must submit yourself to something greater than yourself. You need to be able to go to God and say 'I can't do this on my own. I need help.'

"It's very difficult for us to appear weak. It's even more difficult to have to admit it. It's a source of embarrassment in today's world. So as people endure their struggles with temptation, anger, jealousy, lust, addictions, and every other obstacle life can throw at us, we become very discouraged. Because more times than not, we end up losing these battles. Now, you may be forced to look at yourself as a weak person who couldn't overcome and beat this problem. Some may even see themselves as a failure—something nobody wants to consider themselves to be. So, what's the end result from all of this? We end up indulging even more in the very thing we were trying to overcome! We convince ourselves that it's okay so we don't have to face the reality of our failures.

"People are victims of indifferentism. They don't want to know what God really wants from them. It's a spiritual laziness!

Most Christians are good Christians. They, for the most part, obey God's laws. They're not bad or evil people, they're just lazy to the spiritual life. They think that showing up to Mass once a week is enough. There's some who pray and even say some rosaries, but that doesn't help you know Christ. Most people don't want to put any effort into their faith, and it shows in how they live their everyday life. How much time is put into God on a daily basis in the average person's life? Practically none. But they have plenty of time for the world. People are never lazy to do something they find enjoyable.

"I won't tell you that living a life following God and His rules is easy. That would be a lie. It's a tremendous amount of work and effort because living a life following God is dying to the world and doing the complete opposite of what the world and society tell you to do. Your whole life is spent being told what to do by a world that can't take care of itself, and people listen to the world. That's the amazing part of it. Hatred, war, prejudice, greed—the list goes on and on.

This is the world we take our way of life from! It's beyond a person's understanding to turn their back on the world, and live a life following Christ. It takes a very strong person to do that—something that is very rare. But if we would receive Jesus on a more frequent basis, ah, now we have something to fight back with.

"Pope Pius X said, 'If you receive Holy Communion daily or regularly, it's almost impossible to commit mortal sin.' That is a very powerful thought. Let's not forget that if you die in a state of mortal sin, you will not be saved. Our Lord makes that very clear to us. But most people walk around every day not even aware that they're in a state of mortal sin. Most don't even know what mortal sin is! The average person is completely unprepared to meet God in judgment.

"When a person dies suddenly of a heart attack, car accident, or whatever, we always say 'What a tragedy.' But the real tragedy is that they're not prepared to meet God. They're going to go before God to answer for every thought, word, and action of their lives and won't have any defense whatsoever. That's a tragedy!

"Now there's two sides to this because there are those who do receive Holy Communion daily, but are they doing it out of love for God or has it just become another part of their routine? You must understand the true wonder of what you're partaking in. And if you can, boy will your life change!

"I have asked many people over the years, 'What do you say to God once you've received Him?' They generally look at me very puzzled. The normal answer is 'I say this prayer or that prayer.' Well, that's all fine and good, but those are someone else's prayers. What do you want to say to God?

"People have a hard time relating to Jesus as a person that they can talk to. They think of praying as scripted, structured prayers, which are fine. There's nothing wrong with saying prayers like the rosary or the Our Father, but that's not developing an intimate relationship with Jesus.

"You've come up to receive Jesus, He is now physically inside of you, and you have nothing to say to Him! Is your life going so perfect that you don't need to approach our Lord with your problems and ask for help? And if everything is going well, shouldn't you thank Him for that because life could be dealing you some real tragedy instead? If things are good, it's because God is bestowing His graces upon you. Don't be so arrogant to think that it's you that's arranged things so well in your life. You'd better believe that it can be taken away from you at any moment. I don't know about you, but I would be deathly afraid to think that highly of myself.

"Holy Communion is Heavenly Food". Just as the body needs food to survive, the soul needs the same nourishment. It's only through daily or frequent reception of this Heavenly Food that our souls will begin to grow and draw closer to Jesus every time we receive Him.

"Think about it: the creator of all living things, of the universe, and everything in it can be physically within you if you want. That is some gift! But what kind of preparation are people putting into receiving our Lord? It seems like very little. They arrive at church and chat with the people they haven't seen since last week. The last thing on their mind is shutting everyone out, lowering their head in prayer, and attempting to grasp the unbelievable event that's about to take place in their lives. Look around the church and see who's immersed in prayer and contemplation. Practically nobody. They're talking, reading the weekly bulletin, everything but trying to get closer to Jesus. You're about to receive God! I'll bet my life nobody's even thinking about it. It couldn't mean less. It's just another part of their weekly routine. Have you ever seen anybody receive communion, and then out the door they go?"

"Sure, I have. Plenty of times," I answer.

"Of course, we all have. They have no concept of what's just happened to them. It means practically nothing, but I went to church this week. I fulfilled my obligation. I'm such a good Catholic. What if you came over here every day, walked in the door, sat down, and said to me, 'Hi, how are you?' Then turned around and left. How would we get to know each other?"

"I guess, we wouldn't. It would be a very artificial relationship," I say.

"Exactly! Most have no idea how to have a relationship with Christ. When you receive our Lord, you have to try and connect yourself with Him. Try not to get distracted and stop looking around. Instead of saying a Hail Mary, try talking to Jesus about your life, your fears, concerns, happiness, whatever. We need to develop a personal relationship with Christ. Most people have never even considered doing this. It's all about saying structured prayers. Few people practice mental prayer.

"When you receive Holy Communion, make a proper thanksgiving. You want to talk about offending God, receive Him and don't give proper thanks. It'll be an offense you don't want to answer for, believe me. When you make a proper thanksgiving, you'll begin to develop an intimate relationship with God. You will begin to literally fall in love with Him, and that's what He wants from us. If you love Christ, you're not going to want to sin. It would sicken you to even think about it because you know that if you do, you will offend Him. If you truly love somebody, you go out of your way not to hurt or offend them. Daily communion will give you all the things you need. It will provide the tools for developing that intimate relationship with Christ. It will draw you closer to Him, and open up a world that you never thought could be possible."

Our Lady of Sorrows Chapel

Chapter 3

Mental Prayer

"That all makes perfect sense, Father. Since I started receiving communion daily, I approach my problems in a much different way. But mental prayer is a little difficult for me. I'm so used to structured prayers that just turning to Jesus in conversation seems very foreign to me."

"You're not unique in that way. Most people don't understand anything about mental prayer," Father says.

"I'll bet if you ask the average Christian if they've ever heard the term *mental prayer*, they wouldn't know what you're talking about. I've been asking people for decades when they come to me with a problem or in confession, 'How's your mental prayer life?' They don't know what to say. Mental prayer should be an intricate part of everyone's life, and there's so many opportunities to practice mental prayer. But do you know what I've heard from most people over the years about prayer, either structured or mental?"

"What?" I ask.

"'I don't have the time,' they say. I mean, are you kidding me? There's so many times during your day that you can be immersed in mental prayer. It could be something quick, like when you're brushing your teeth, driving to work or the store, or bringing the kids to school. What do people do when they get in their cars?"

"They put on the radio," I answer.

"Exactly. Sounds like a great opportunity to talk to God. Unfortunately, most people can't be bothered. People are so distracted by the world, they don't even think about developing a relationship with God outside of church. But how many are trying to develop a relationship with Him when in church? Sadly, most are just there.

Mental prayer is so important that without it you're completely lost in your spiritual life. I've known so many people who revolve their day around saying the rosary. They say rosary after rosary. Now the rosary is a beautiful and very powerful prayer, but it can become systematic. Also, how many people are doing what they're supposed to be doing during the rosary which is heartfully meditating on each mystery? It becomes very mechanical, and it gets people to the point where their only concern is getting their rosary in. It's of no benefit to pray without your heart and mind deep in your prayers. You can say a hundred rosaries a day, but if your hearts not in it, then you're wasting your time. People have a hard time understanding that. All they care about is 'I prayed my rosaries today.' Great, but how much closer to God did they bring you?

"When I was a teenager, I prayed seven rosaries a day. It was my routine. When I entered the Trappist monastery at eighteen, the abbot or the head of the monastery, told me to stop praying so many rosaries. I was shocked! I thought, 'No way, I have to pray my rosaries.' He told me, instead of saying so many rosaries, to go outside, take a walk, sit down, and just talk to our Lord. I thought, 'Okay, but I need to say my rosaries.'

"Now you've been up to the Trappist monastery with me, and you've seen the two thousand acres of land they have and how peaceful and beautiful it is. So, I did what the abbot said. I took a walk and sat down under a tree and just started talking to God, just like I'm sitting here talking to you. The next thing I knew, a couple of hours had passed. I couldn't believe how quickly the time went by and how close I felt to our Lord.

"I never knew that praying could make you feel so close to God, and that's because I didn't relate talking to God as praying. I thought that rosaries and novenas, etc. were the only ways to pray, but that's absolutely wrong.

"The definition of prayer, according to The Baltimore Catechism, is 'the lifting of the heart and mind to God.' That's it. You don't have to recite set prayers all the time. Just being aware of our Lord is a form of praying. I can sometimes be in the busiest of places—a grocery store or the shopping mall—where there's people and noise everywhere and feel completely alone and not notice anyone around me because I'm thinking about Jesus and knowing that He's there with me. Everyone and everything around me just seems to fade into the background because I'm so aware of the presence of God there with me. That's praying!

"You can say tons of structured prayers, written prayers, but they'll never get you as close to God as just being aware of Him and focusing in on that. When you can do that, you will begin to develop a deep, spiritual, and lasting relationship with our Lord. And while all three things: frequent Holy Communion, mental prayer, and spiritual reading are all equally important, if you had to focus on one to start your true spiritual journey to a relationship with God, I'd say focus on mental prayer most because it will draw you to Him constantly and you can do it as often as you wish.

"Don't misunderstand me. Praying the rosary, novenas, and other structured prayers are wonderful things to do. Praying the rosary is a means of drawing yourself closer to Christ through Mary. It's essential in a good prayer life, but don't limit yourself to just those prayers. The goal is intimacy with Christ, and you can only achieve that by speaking personally to Him. If you want to develop a closer, more personal relationship with God, you must talk to Him.

"It's no different than developing a relationship with anybody else in your life. The only way to get to know somebody is to spend time with them and talk with them, hence, daily communion and mental prayer. It's all very simple, these are just things that most people don't know to do or don't care to do.

"When people say to me that they have no time to pray, it makes me nuts. I bet they have time to sit on their computer and look at Facebook. How much time is spent texting with their friends about nothing important? And I bet they won't miss their favorite TV program tonight, but 'I have no time for God today.' Well, let me tell you. When you don't have time for God, He doesn't have time for you, either, and I can assure you that you'll need Him more than He'll need you.

"Not only that, but mental prayer is so peaceful and beautiful. You're developing a wonderful relationship with God. How awesome is that? He will be a better friend to you than anybody you've ever known has been. I can guarantee you that.

"Think about the best friend you've ever known in your life and how wonderful you feel when you're with them, and even after you're done spending time with them that day, you go home feeling so good about the wonderful relationship you have with that person. We should be striving daily to develop that kind of relationship with God. He's there waiting for you to come and talk to Him every day.

"If we're here to know, love, and serve God, then the only way to do that is to get to know Him. If you don't have the desire to spend time with God now, what makes you think you'll want to spend eternity with him? Most people deceive themselves into thinking that they love God and want to go to Heaven. They say they do, but those are just words. If they actually meant it, they would be striving daily to get closer to Him. And again, how can that be accomplished?"

"By daily communion and mental prayer," I respond.

"Exactly! It's impossible to love God if you don't know Him, just like it's impossible to love anybody here on Earth without knowing them. Again, part of the problem is that most people don't relate to God as someone they can interact with intimately, as someone they can just talk to. He's almost like a celebrity that you would be too nervous to approach if you ran into them on the street. He's this figure that's so much greater than we are and so far above us that we can't relate to Him. But the truth is, He's right here on our level, just waiting for us to approach Him with the smallest concern.

"People have convinced themselves that they can't associate directly with God, partly because they think they're so unworthy of Him, and that's true. We are unworthy of Him. He is so perfect and we are so lowly and sinful, but that's the beauty of God's love and mercy for us—that he's willing to come down to our level, to be there and listen to our most insignificant problems at any time. If people could only understand that each one of us is so important to Him, so precious in His eyes, they would work tirelessly to develop a personal relationship with Him through mental prayer. I feel bad for people who don't understand this because they're missing out on the single greatest relationship of their earthly lives."

"Everything you're saying makes sense, Father, but I think part of the problem is that people have a hard time developing a relationship with somebody that isn't there in front of them. I know that He's physically present in the tabernacle, but I think that's a hard thing for people to understand and build a relationship on."

"True, it is hard to grasp the concept of God being there physically like a person, but isn't that part of faith? It can also take some time. Often, people get discouraged because they don't feel like they're getting closer to God right away. It's no different than the years it took you to develop the relationship you have with your wife. It's not quick, but like everything with God, it comes through patience and perseverance. The key is not to give up. Remember, 'He that shall persevere to the end, shall be saved' (Matthew 24:13).

"We have to stop letting the things of the world consume all of our thoughts. Nobody wants peace and quiet. They constantly need the noise and distractions of the world. I'm not sure why that is, but it's true. Who do you know that goes off somewhere without their cell phone and just spends an hour or so in quiet time talking to God or spending a little time away from the world? A church can be so quiet and filled with spirituality, yet it seems that very few stop by their parish church to just sit there for a little while and reflect on things. They'd rather be out in the world with all its chaos than to be a recluse for a little while. People seem to enjoy the problems and drama that goes along with a worldly life. They complain plenty about their lives, but few make any efforts to make positive changes in it.

"Spending time in mental prayer will open your mind to ways of thinking that are more meaningful than the world's ways. It will allow God to talk to you, and you'll be able to understand Him because you won't be distracted by the hectic things around you. It does require some effort on our part to make a decision and turn the world off for a little while—something most people refuse to do.

"If people would only understand the value of a good mental prayer life, they would see drastic changes in their lives. It would raise them to a level of peace and fulfillment that they've never known before. God will respond if you just stop for a while, open your heart and mind, and let Him in. It's one of the most important things we can do if we truly want to secure our spot in Heaven. Perhaps, people should do a thorough self-examination to find out if going to Heaven is what they truly want or is it just something they say they're interested in.

Here's the truth, practically nobody goes directly to Heaven, and if someone is telling you that you will, whoever it is, you should stop talking to them immediately because they are going to help lead you directly to Hell. If you truly desire Heaven, then you'll have to make some serious changes in the way you live your life. You must realize that being a good person isn't nearly sufficient in obtaining the goal of Heaven. It's what Jesus, the prophets, saints, mystics, and visionaries of the church have always taught. People who could perform miracles were blessed with the stigmata and had direct interactions with Christ all taught the same thing—those who go directly to Heaven are so few that it can be counted on your fingers. We must stop listening to the world and open ourselves to the true teachings of Christ.

"We must allow God into our lives through mental prayer. If we do, God will bring us closer to Him, and we can release ourselves from this burden of trying to figure out what to do in our lives. Just like a good friend would give you the best advice they can to try and direct you, through mental prayer, God will bestow His graces on you to help guide you on your way. Trust in God and listen to your heart when you're immersed in mental prayer and what God is trying to tell you. How can we go wrong if we trust in God?"

Chapter 4

Spiritual Reading

"It's pretty impressive how St. Benedict was able to recognize these things that can draw us to Christ," I say.

"Yes, he was very wise and understood the importance of a personal relationship with God and how to obtain it. The thing is, you need all three together," Father responds.

"Consider spiritual reading. There's much to learn from the saints who have given us direct insight into God. Before each Mass, we always read a brief summary of the life of the saint for that day, how amazing were their lives, and the severe trials they went through for the love of Christ.

"The saints have given us so much to learn from and reflect on. So many of these saints had very personal and intimate encounters with Christ. They had visions and could perform miracles. Most people have no idea about the saints. Sure, they know a few saints like St. Francis or St. Teresa the little flower, but that's about it. And shame on any Catholic who doesn't know about these amazing people who, many of them, gave their lives for the Church and for love of God. There are countless numbers of saints and martyrs in the church, and most people today don't know about any of them and they don't care to know any of them. But ask them about that fifty colors of gray book, or whatever it's called, or about Harry Potter, and they can tell you every detail. How sad!

"Imagine if God blessed you with the ability to have visions of Heaven or Hell, or to be blessed with the stigmata, or being able to perform miracles. It's happened so many times to so many saints. And if you ask the average Catholic to name any, you'd be lucky if they could name one! How extremely sad.

"This is all part of knowing your faith. Do you think God blessed these people with those abilities because He was bored and had nothing else better to do? He did it so we could have firm belief and faith in Him and Heaven. So we would have a constant reminder of how to live our lives for serving Him every day, not just for an hour on Sunday.

"For centuries, the church was being built by these people—the popes and saints—who worked tirelessly every day at serving God and doing His will. They have left us all the information we need to have a perfect understanding of what God demands from us and our earthly lives. But if nobody is reading and studying their faith, how are they going to know what to do?

"There is no excuse whatsoever for people not knowing their faith. It's all right here in front of us just waiting to be read, absorbed, and put into use in our lives, but who's doing that? Show me how many Catholic homes have some books on the lives of the saints? If they're there, I'm sure they're collecting dust.

"Apparently, people don't find learning about God, His church, or the people He has chosen specially to give testimony of Him, very exciting. Of course, if it had brazen sex and murder in it, they wouldn't be able to put it down. The average Catholic probably owns a Bible that they rarely look at, let alone a book on the saints. It's just not something that occurs to most people. What's your favorite book?"

"Easy. The Imitation of Christ. I've read it dozens of times and still read a few pages every day," I respond.

"Me, too. By far the greatest book into the spiritual life ever written. Pope Pius XII called it 'the greatest book next to the Bible,' and he's right! That book can literally change your life and lead you on your path to Heaven. But if you ask most people, especially Catholics, if they've ever heard of it, you'll get the same answer—no! That's amazing to me. A book that gives you perfect insight into a proper and healthy spiritual life and most people have never heard of it.

"You can see what priorities people have by what they read. A book on love, lust, and sex will keep them busy for hours, but a book that can help them save their soul couldn't draw any less attention. Perhaps people should ask themselves which book can lead them to Heaven.

"Think of all the great saints of the church. They all have a story. It's an amazing way to learn what to do to live in union with Christ. They've already done the work for us. All we have to do is read about it and imitate it. Of course, if you look around the average person's home you won't find many books on the faith.

"I think people have it in their head that they can figure out what to do to serve God on their own, and that will be good enough. However, we know that's not the case, and the wreck that many people's lives are in proves that they can't do it on their own. But most people are so wrapped up in themselves they can't see that they may need help. God has given us a road map to Heaven by blessing the saints with tremendous gifts. Those gifts were given to them so we would know what to do to earn eternal salvation.

"People get too caught up in the world to differentiate their everyday life from their spiritual life. They try to incorporate the two together, and they get discouraged because it doesn't work. The reason it doesn't work is because your spiritual life can't be of the world, it has to be of God. The world will never mix with God, so we must rely on the saints to guide us through our lives while staying close to Jesus. Without that help and direction from the saints, we're lost.

"It's complete arrogance on the part of most people because they think they've got their lives completely under control. Now if their lives were truly *under control* the way they believe them to be, then why would they seek out priests or therapists on a regular basis to try and correct the state their lives are realistically in? For nearly forty years, people have been coming to me regularly, and I would suspect most priests as well, in tears about their marriage, job, children, or whatever! They come to us looking for a magical solution to their problems, and when we give them advice of a spiritual nature on how to start correcting their lives by doing things like receiving Holy Communion more frequently or developing their prayer life, they seem to reject that advice. Most people want to hear a solution from the world. It simply makes more sense to them.

"What most fail to understand is that giving up control of your life and problems, and allowing God to navigate for you will correct any problems you may have. Developing your prayer life, receiving Holy Communion, working through your problems with patience, humility, rationalization, and thought not emotions will put your life directly into place. If a person had to be honest, and I mean truly honest, within themselves about the state of their marriage, how many could say it's successful and they are truly happy? The blank look on your face speaks volumes! I'm going to tell you the biggest problem in every marriage. Are you ready? Pride. That's it, just pride. Nobody is willing to concede to the other one. 'You have to agree with me. I'm right, you're wrong. End of story.' The problem is, both people have the same attitude and nothing ever gets resolved. Where is humility? It doesn't matter if you're right or wrong, practice humility! Jesus didn't do anything wrong. All the accusations against Him were false, but He stood there in humility and accepted it to the point of death! Yet people are having arguments over dinner?

"Oh, how people deceive themselves when they say they live a life in communion with Christ. I can count on one hand the amount of people who have taken my advice about their relationships. Obviously, people think very little about the power and influence God can have in their life. Perhaps they should seek their advice elsewhere, rather than with a priest.

"What happens when a person seeks a therapist's help? More times than not, they end up taking some kind of pills. This is not a cure. It's a temporary solution to a problem that lies within the heart, mind, and soul. If you think you'll lead a happier life by taking pills rather than receiving Holy Communion and praying to our Lord, then good luck.

"Letting someone else, like the saints, guide your decisions and way through life takes a tremendous amount of humility—something we lack in today's world. It's looking to something greater, smarter, or perhaps better than you are, and saying 'Okay, I'm struggling here and I can use some help and direction.' That's exactly what the saints offer us because they've traveled the road we're on now, and many of them did it with direct blessings from God. How can we not follow their examples and ways? It'll only help us ensure our own salvation.

"People put too much importance on their own opinions and ways of thinking. It takes a person who truly wants to be in love with God to say 'Please, help me,' and turn to the saints through spiritual reading to gain that understanding.

"Not only can you learn how the saints lived their lives, but spiritual reading will help you learn your faith. Most people don't know anything about their religion, and I mean the most basic things. Ask the average Christian some questions about the faith. They won't have many answers for you. What if you're in a conversation with someone of a different faith, how can you defend your beliefs if you don't know anything about it? There is so much that can be gained from spiritual reading. Sadly, most people's interest doesn't lie in their faith, it lies in the world.

"The same excuses come up over and over when I talk to people about doing spiritual reading, 'I don't have the time.' That's such crap! How many hours a night does a person spend in front of their TV? You can't take a lousy fifteen minutes to read a little about God, the one who's supposed to be so important to you? People sure are liars when they say they love God.

"We are obliged to know our faith. Consider it a wonderful gift to be able to gain insight into God, His saints, and the beauty that is your faith through spiritual reading. This is how we're supposed to live our lives, not for the world but for God.

The more you choose the world and the less you say yes to God the more likely you are to hear those dreaded words at your particular judgment. 'Depart from me, you cursed, into everlasting fire which was prepared for the devil and his angels' (Matthew 25:41).'"

Rectory sitting area

Chapter 5

The World

"You know, Father, I can't understand why people have such a hard time doing the things that will obviously help them get to Heaven."

"I've been wondering that for years myself. The biggest obstacle in people's lives is the world itself. The world is a huge distraction to the spiritual life. We're taught from a very young age to love the world, not God. God has little place in society today, and it's fairly obvious that He doesn't by looking at the state the world is in. If people put God first in their lives, there wouldn't be many of the problems we see today. People are so wrapped up in themselves and their own self-importance that they can't possibly conceive anything else.

"People seek pleasure in their lives. It's all they want because that's what the world tells them to seek out. God teaches us the exact opposite. He tells us that this life is for suffering and trials, who wants that? Consider what our Blessed Mother said to St. Bernadette at Lourdes, 'I cannot promise you happiness in this world, only in the next.'

"We want to be happy and comfortable every minute of our day. It's become so bad that when difficult things happen to people, they can't handle it. They put so much time and energy into creating a perfect little world for themselves and shutting out anything negative, but you can't do that because there's always something opposing happening in our lives.

"You would think people might realize that this is the way things are supposed to be. No matter how hard we try, nothing ever goes the way we plan. There's always something that gets screwed up, why? One reason is because we try to decide what is best for us, and perhaps God has another plan. Another reason may be, is that God is testing our patience. We are constantly having our patience tested by God. He wants to see how we'll handle things. If we have so little patience now, how will we survive the torments of purgatory? Our society has become one of impatience. We want what we want, when we want it, and how we want it. How arrogant of us to have such expectations! Who are we to demand such things?

"People have convinced themselves that the only way to be happy is to have lots of stuff. The world is full of cool stuff, but that's temporary satisfaction. We seek the things that we think will make our lives better. However, I've never seen anybody's life become better by driving a BMW or having a mansion. Whether you're driving a $100,000 car or a $10,000 car, just be happy you have a way to get around. But no, the cheaper isn't good enough. Besides, what will my neighbor think if I'm driving a lesser car than him? He might think I'm not as successful as he is, and I can't have that.

"People are so concerned with what others think, they'll actually base their decisions on another's opinion. How many people buy a car or house they really can't afford just so people will think they can afford it? It's such twisted logic, but that's what the world has made of us. There's so much pride and vanity within ourselves. People try to make themselves into the person they conceive themselves to be. Unfortunately, that never works.

"The truly sad part about the whole thing is that the one person they should be making every effort to impress is God. But who thinks that way? Total strangers play a larger part in a person's life than God does. We search so hard to try to find just a moment of happiness. People work hard all year, save their money, and put all sorts of effort into something like a vacation. They pack their bags, spend hours traveling, wait in lines for attractions, etc. But for eternal salvation, people will scarcely lift a finger. The values and priorities of most are completely out of whack!

"'There's a very scary but true statement from the New Testament. 'It is a fearful thing to fall into the hands of the living God' (Hebrews 10:31). Wow! How true that is. When we die and go before the judgment seat of God, we are going to see ourselves for who we really are. In an instant, you will have a perfect understanding of yourself and the life you've led—both the good you've done and the evil. At that moment, you will realize that your lifelong efforts of striving for the things of the world were pointless and unimportant. You'll also know at that moment, the one thing that was truly important—loving God—is now something that is too late to try to develop. You'll see how you allowed the devil and the world to control your life and most of your decisions. And if you hear the judgment of God casting you into everlasting fire, you'll know that it was your own stubbornness and ignorance that has sent you there. There will be absolutely no one to blame for your damnation but yourself, and you will have eternity to regret your worldly ways.

"People put a tremendous amount of importance on their thoughts, opinions, and beliefs. They think they know so much and have convinced themselves that their thoughts are reality: 'I think this way, so it must be so.'

"All of the things I'm sitting here telling you are not my opinions, they're church teachings. Since the age of nine, I have not just read about the Christian faith but studied very carefully the Christian faith. These were the things Christ taught while here on Earth. They're the things that the popes and great saints have understood, written down, and taught us for centuries, except for the present time because the teachings of the church today are in complete contradiction to actual Catholic teachings—one more thing nobody wants to acknowledge. I don't offer my opinion, ever! I have read more books than I can count, and have spent my life doing exactly what the Lord and the church have taught. There's one more thing I can tell you with absolute certainty, and that is that Christ did not teach the embrace of modernism. In fact, He taught the exact opposite. So, beware all who think they can modernize the church. Believe me when I tell you that if you live your life in union with the world, you may perish in Hell for eternity.

"The world is a very deceitful place, and people don't realize that their indifference to God is actually paving their road to Hell. You see how little time and thought most people give to God. Going to church once a week isn't going to do it. Saying a rosary every day isn't going to be sufficient. You must put God before all things and love Him above all things. How many people can you show me today who live this way?

"Most people are interested in living for themselves and what makes them happy at that moment. They couldn't care less about what God wants from them. They think they care and they think they live their lives for God, but they're really living for the world. The average person is good in the eyes of the world, not God. People miss the fact that God's standards are much different than the world's standards. Being a good person and following the rules of society have nothing to do with God. You're a sinful person in the eyes of the Lord, and people refuse to understand that because then they would have to make some profound changes in their ways of thinking and living. The average person can't fathom that they're sinful in the eyes of God because they live what they believe to be a good life, but they're living a good life to society's ways, not God's.

"The world tells us every day how to live our lives. TV, movies, and radio do nothing but draw you to the pleasures and distractions of the world. Do you really think God wants you going out of your way to go lay on a beach on some island? You can't seek rest in this life, then expect to be rewarded with eternal rest in Heaven. It doesn't work that way. People don't think. Every decision they make is for the world!

"God's interest doesn't lie in your happiness here on earth. That's reserved for Heaven. You'll often hear people say 'God wants us to be happy.' True, He does, but not with worldly things. The happiness God wants for you is that you turn to and trust Him with every situation in your life. Say, you're homeless, stricken with a deadly disease, suffering the greatest, unjust cruelty this world has to offer, or rejoicing in the wonderful luxuries you may have, then you turn to God and say 'Thank you' for Him bestowing on you whatever He sees fit. How many people do you know that could lose every material thing they have—job, house, car, etc.—and turn to God and say 'Thank you?' Nobody is the answer, and why? Because these are all things the world says you need to have happiness. Consider hermits—they left everything they had, went into the desert, and lived their lives alone and without any possessions for the love of God, and they were thankful to God to do it. That's the happiness God gives to us, not in material possessions.

"Most of our efforts revolve around gaining the material things that bring us joy. Do you really think God wants you driving a luxury car, having a big beautiful home; to have boats, motorcycles and other toys? Really! This is what you think God wants for us? This life is for battling through temptations, trials. and sufferings, giving thanks and glory to Jesus for what He's given to us—the opportunity of spending eternity in Heaven with Him, and not enjoying the things that man has come up with to please us. It's not that these things are bad or evil, it's that they've become more important to our lives than God. People are so involved with material things, they think it's just a part of life. What they haven't considered is the source of their fortunes. God is the reason for all the wonderful things you may have in your life, and He can take it away at any time. If you're so fortunate to have many of the things you desire, it would be wise to give thanks to the one who provided it to you.

"God has been so far removed from society that when you say to people it's better to sit home in prayer than to go outside and have fun, they look at you like you should be locked up. I hear the same thing over and over, 'I work hard, I deserve some rest and fun.' No, you don't. You deserve to crawl in front of our Lord and beg His forgiveness for your sins. But people don't think they sin because the world has told them that as long as you're a good person you're okay. Well, let me tell you that at the end of your life it won't be the world judging you, it will be God, and going before Him with a life spent enjoying what the world offered you and not what God offered, can be an assured judgment of damnation, and you will have chosen that judgment, not God."

Chapter 6

Misconceptions

"Sometimes I feel bad for people because they're going through their lives thinking that everything is okay with the way they live. Part of it's their fault, and part of it's not."

"What do you mean?" I ask.

"Well, people go to church and should get direction and understanding from their priests on how to live and what they should and should not be doing to make their way to Heaven. However, many priests today seem only interested in telling people things that will make them feel good. They don't want anybody walking out after Mass unhappy or feeling sad.

"Do you know how many times I've had people so upset at me for my sermons on how their way of life can put them in Hell? I've had people who simply stopped coming to Mass because they didn't like what I had to say, and why? Because the reality I present to them forces them to do some thinking, and they don't like the thought of maybe having to make some changes.

"I've said it before, people want to live the way they want to live and that's it! Nobody is going to tell them differently, even God. So, a lot of priests today fluff everything up and encourage good behavior and the basics of being a good person: help others, be kind, try to act like Jesus, etc. Those are all fine things, but they won't get you to Heaven!

"People are looking for guidance from their priests but often get watered-down information instead. They could, however, do their own spiritual studying and find these things out on their own, but not many do that. As a matter of fact, who tries to do the very few things that are being taught each week by their parish priests? Believe me, the moment a sermon is over, most people's minds are instantly somewhere else. They're not concerned with what they've just heard because they can't conceive that how they're living might need improvement.

"It seems that change is hard for most. It's not that people are living badly, they simply don't understand what's required of salvation. And apparently, many priests today don't understand, either. We listen to what the world has to say these days, not God. We're so attached to the things of the world, our material possessions, pride, the belief that we know what's best for us, and so on. When a person has a problem and turns to prayer, what do they say? They ask God to give them what they want. Did it ever occur to you that what you want may not be the best thing for you? And if they don't get what they ask for, look out! 'God has abandoned me.' 'He doesn't care about me.' What pride and arrogance we have.

"The world has taught us that we should know what's best for us, so now we know better than God? People baffle me! Look at the decisions people make in their lives. If your life isn't exactly working out the way you want it to, it's more than likely due to the decisions you've made about the course of your life. When you have a problem, it's best to turn to Jesus or whatever saint you may have a devotion to, and say, 'I place this problem in your hands,' and that's it. Does God want something bad for us? Is He going to lead you down the wrong road? Of course not. Would you do that to your child? God only wants what's best for us. The problem with this is that we lack patience. We want our prayers answered now! I hate to say it but everything is in God's time, not ours. Have you ever prayed for something and didn't get it which made you upset? We all have. Then maybe a few months go by and something even better happens and you think to yourself, 'I'm so happy what I asked for wasn't answered or I wouldn't have this now.' Our lack of patience and trust in God robs us of such peace in our lives. If we could just realize that, our lives would be so much easier.

"'Seek ye first the kingdom of God and His approval and all things will be given to you' (Matthew 6:33). That means putting God first in all things—turning to God instead of the world, increasing your prayer life, not watching TV all the time, etc. If we can do this, we would have all we want and then some. Unfortunately, most can't do this. We're so caught up in ourselves and our self-importance that we would never consider not managing our own problems. We need control of our own lives. 'God doesn't know what's best for me, I do. God just needs to provide it.'

"People use God like a magician. When things are bad, they turn to Him for help. How many times do you see people come here to church that you've never seen before and will never see again? They have a problem and come here to ask for *their* solution, and then go away. Sometimes they ask me to say a Mass or give them a blessing, and that's it. You can't choose to call on God when it's convenient for you and ignore Him the rest of the time. It just doesn't work that way. But in people's selfishness, they think that's the way it should be. And when it doesn't work, God doesn't care about me.

"This is completely unreasonable thinking on our parts. God is not a magic tool to be called on when you need a favor. The only way to obtain the things we need from God is through prayer and faithfulness to Him daily. Notice I said *need,* not *want.*

"We want so many things we don't need, but God isn't interested in excess. Look at the way Jesus lived—He was poor and had nothing. Are you better than God? Are you entitled to luxuries when our Lord could sometimes not even find a place to lay His head? Who are we to demand such privilege and luxury in our lives?

"God came to earth in the form of a man to teach us by His example humility and simplicity, to serve God with patience and faith, yet we have turned His examples into our own self-righteous ways to demand things we have convinced ourselves we are entitled to. We are entitled to nothing! We should consider ourselves of such little value. To think we are good or have something to offer God is preposterous.

"From the moment we wake up in the morning until the time we close our eyes and fall asleep, we are constantly offending God by our thoughts, words, and actions. People think they're so good, they're walking around in a state of delusion thinking that God must be so happy with them. If we could only see ourselves for who we really are! Let me tell you how utterly shocked people are going to be at their judgment when God shows them all the ways they've offended Him on a daily basis. That's why so few go to confession regularly. They're not even aware of their sins or what sin is, for that matter. How can people expect to be in a state of grace, which is required at the time of death to be saved, when they don't even understand how they commit sin?

"People have made the grave mistake of taking God for granted. We think all we have to do is lead a good life, and the gates of Heaven will be opened to us. You hear it every time somebody dies. 'Well, they're in a better place now.' No, they're not! As a matter of fact, there's a good chance they're in hell! They lived a worldly life, gave none or the bare minimum of their time to God and in loving and serving Him. They don't know Jesus at all and had no relationship with Him, but they're in Heaven? No way!

"Wake up and face reality! You can't live a worldly life and expect to be saved. People actually think they deserve to be saved. Deserve it! Are you kidding me? We deserve Hell—every one of us. There isn't one person on the planet, you and I included, who hasn't offended God to the point that they deserve anything less than Hell, and anyone who doesn't think they deserve Hell is fooling themselves, and that goes for everyone!

"We deserve nothing good in this life, only to bear our trials patiently for the love of God and to accept the sufferings He bestows on us with joy and gratitude. God owes us nothing. We do, however, owe God everything, and we will pay what we owe at our judgment."

Chapter 7

Who Is God?

"The problem today, and I would suspect for most of history, is that most people don't know God, they know the world. They're living in the world, and therefore, that's what they know.

"I spent many years away from the world in monasteries. The difference in a person's life there and a person's life in the world is amazing. In the monastery, your daily life revolves around God. Everything you do has God at the center of it. In the world, you can barely find a trace of God. People strive so hard to obtain the things of the world. They work so hard for a house or car, but nobody seems to put any work into God. While we all need a roof over our heads, we don't need the elaborate houses that we kill ourselves to afford. All of these earthly luxuries seem so empty in my eyes. I couldn't imagine not putting my main efforts into loving and serving God every day, shouldn't that be our main focus?

"I'm not saying we shouldn't work hard at our jobs and create a comfortable living environment for ourselves and our families, but it shouldn't become top priority. Remember, God can take anything away from you He wants at any time. To work hard for material gain alone seems so fruitless. One of the greatest gifts you can give God is to get up every morning and do your job for the glory of God, and you can do that by giving it 100% every day. By doing it without complaint, especially if you're stuck in a job that you hate or have coworkers that you don't get along with. But to do it for material gain alone, how futile! Every day on your way to work, say to God, 'Lord, I offer this entire day's labor up to you. The good I perform or the evil I may endure,

I offer it to you in reparation for my sins.' What a pleasing gift to God this will be.

"When I chose to become a Trappist at eighteen, my mother was the only one who supported my decision, the rest of my family and my friends thought I was nuts! They said, 'What a wasted life that will be.' Their idea of success was having money and the possessions that go with it. That, to me, was an empty life. I saw the unhappiness that went along with the obsession of material gain by watching the marriages of my friends' parents and my own parents end in disaster. The constant fighting and arguing with each other made no sense to me. Plus, you always heard them complaining about the people they worked with or the person down the street that they now have a problem with. Why would people want to live in that constant state of arguing and tension? It's just a way of life that's never made any sense to me.

"When I reentered the world, I saw how miserable everybody's lives seemed to be. Sure, they had their material possessions, but none of them had peace and happiness. They all seemed to be in unhappy marriages and complained about their lives constantly. They didn't know a happy day in their lives. Meanwhile, I was so happy with the life I was living. My dedication to God had fulfilled every need I could possibly desire, yet they were still critical of my choice. I had known twenty years of constant peace and serenity in the monastery, yet everybody looked at me as if I'd missed out on such a fulfilling life in the world. What most haven't figured out is that the world and God are two separate things, and no matter how hard you try, they cannot be mixed together.

"Most people don't know who God is. They go to church weekly and live a good and moral life. Because of this, they have subconsciously convinced themselves that they know and love God but they don't really know Him or how to serve Him. Many pick and choose the way they're going to follow God. They have their own ideas and opinions about how to live that works for their living situation. Even if their way of life differs from the teachings of Jesus and the church, they convince themselves that what they're doing is okay.

"One thing that's always shocked me is having a Christian come to me and ask if it's okay to have an abortion. I've had this happen to me on several occasions over the years. Have you ever met one of these nuts who think that because the pregnancy isn't of normal or ideal circumstances, the baby should be aborted? It's never okay to abort a child!

"Yes, people who shouldn't have babies are having babies, and I know there's many who disagree with me. but they usually don't call themselves a Christian. How can you possibly justify killing a baby if you believe that the baby was created by God? If you're a Christian, you're obliged to believe it's from the will of God. If you don't, or think under some circumstances that abortion is the answer, you may want to consider another religion.

"The world has affected the decisions we make in our lives in a very negative way. If the world is the answer to your problems, how is God any part of your life? People who've spent their lives going to church weekly and turning to anything other than God for direction are the most ignorant of all! It goes to show how little they pay attention to what's going on in the Mass.

"The teachings of Christ and the church are in contradiction to the world and everything it stands for. It's repeated over and over in the gospels and epistles, yet people do the exact opposite of what the Bible tells us to do. This is because of a lack of trust in God, and because people don't know God, they don't trust in God. Most of peoples' time is put into the things of the world, so why are people going to church every week if they're not going to follow what the church teaches? God has made it very clear to seek Him first in all things and let Him guide us, yet when a problem arises, we become incredibly stressed and don't know what to do. Wouldn't this be the time to seek God and His direction? If you're going to church every week, loving and trusting God the way you claim you are, then why the fear and doubt when a problem surfaces? People deceive themselves into thinking they're living a life following God. If they truly are, then the next time a problem comes up, let's see if they turn to God for the solution.

"It's unfortunate that most people won't take the time to get to know God. Think of Jesus's life—a common guy who ended up performing miracles and dying a most gruesome death. What an amazing story! People get caught up in characters in movies and books. They love this or that about a certain character. How about getting caught up in the things Jesus did? Most know the basics, but there's a lot more to Jesus and His life if you just did a little reading. You don't necessarily have to read the entire Bible because it can be a very difficult book to understand, but there's many books on the life of Jesus that tell an amazing story. There's so much about the life of Jesus that people have no idea about, but He's supposed to be the biggest part of their lives. Oh, how people deceive themselves.

"Most are so in love with the world that they don't want to know God. They'd probably be miserable in Heaven. There is nothing of the world in Heaven. If you're living for the world, why would you want to be somewhere that is the opposite of the world? It's going to be some shock when people die and meet God in judgment and realize that their life spent living for the world is now the thing that's damned their soul.

"People have an attachment to Earthly things—their material possessions, their pride, their own points of view—but these things have no place in Heaven. Loving these things during this life won't change when you die. You're not going to die and suddenly say, 'Oh Jesus, I love you and long to be with you.' They're going to be so attached to the things of this world that it will be unbearable for most to part from them.

"A person truly in love with God will look forward to death, so they can be with Him. But think about dying for a moment, what scares you about it? Is it the loss of the things you are so used to? The fear should be that most people are completely unprepared to meet God in judgment, and that their future may be spent suffering for all of eternity in Hell.

"People have severe indifferentism when it comes to knowing God. It's very common for people to say Jesus is the biggest part of their lives, but is He really? Do people really put Him first in their decisions, views, wants, and desires? People have self-interest at heart, and that's about it. This is proven daily by the decisions people make in their lives, even though it contradicts the teachings of the one they claim is most important to them.

"Consider unwanted pregnancies and abortions. Babies are born every day all over the world to people who can't afford them or simply don't want them. Look at Third World countries where babies die from malnutrition and disease. They don't have enough food to feed themselves, let alone a baby. So, what's the answer to this dilemma? If you ask most people, they'll say 'Well, they're poor. They can't afford contraception, so what are they going to do?' How about not having sex! No, nobody would even consider that. 'I'm going to have sex because it pleases me, and that's more important to me than anything else, including God.'

"The entitlement of people in this world is unbelievable. They truly believe they are owed everything. They believe this because they have no idea who God really is and how to serve Him. It takes a lot of discipline to know God. You must turn your back on the world and the way you've lived your life up until now. It's so important to do, though, because you can't expect to go to Heaven if God isn't first in your life.

"I know the things of the world are enjoyable. They do bring pleasure to us, but it's a brief pleasure. It's not a happiness that's going to last. That's why people are constantly on the lookout for the next thing that can bring them some new enjoyment.

"If they really knew God, they would know true happiness. They wouldn't need to search for it anymore. They would realize that happiness is not found on vacation or in a new car, it's not in a bar or some nightclub. Happiness is in loving the one who will always love you and who will always be there to protect and guide you. The one who will never deceive or let you down. Opening your heart unrestricted to God will give you an understanding of Him, and the peace and love we all desire. Isn't that what we claim we want from this life?"

Chapter 8

Seeking God

"There's only two ways to live; you live for the world or you live for God, and the two can't interact with each other. As scripture says, 'You can't serve God and Mammon (material possessions)' (Luke 16:13).

"It's hard to give up the things of the world to follow God. For most people, it's completely beyond their comprehension, and that's because the world teaches us that more is better, that more is the only way to personal happiness. God teaches us the exact opposite, and it contradicts what people see and hear in their daily lives.

"Now, because people don't spend much time learning their faith or trying to draw closer to God, they forget that He is there waiting for them, ready to give them all that they need if they would seek Him first. But who wants what they need? They want what they want. Most believe that the only way to have something is to get it yourself. Not for a second would they step back and let God do the work. That would take a tremendous amount of faith and trust on our part. Unfortunately, people will only trust themselves to get what they need.

"Seeking God first means to treat everything else in your life as secondary. It means turning to God to find the answers to all your decisions. It's hard for a person not to rely on their own intellect to figure out a problem. That's how we've been taught to handle things our whole lives. With a world so far removed from God, the only thing left is to rely on yourself.

"The problem with this thinking is that you're assuming you know what's right for you. As we know, that doesn't always work out. Right off the bat, people have made the wrong decision because they've chosen to follow the world instead of God. Now if your first decision about how to live was the wrong one, how questionable will the rest of your decisions be?

"We're so quick to trust ourselves, and I don't understand why. People don't seem to look at their past mistakes and learn from them, they seem to repeat the same behavior over and over. They're relying on themselves and not God. They don't stop and think about how they continually end up in the same place with the same results. If it didn't work the last time, what makes you think it'll work this time? This is exactly what the devil wants from us—he wants us to keep trying in the world and seeking after it more and more. When people are trying to achieve something and it doesn't work, they look at themselves as a failure. Perhaps God is trying to tell them 'This is not right for you.' Our minds need to open to God and His direction, and we need to trust in that and not get upset when it doesn't go our way.

"Now, I'm not saying that people should abandon their lives. They shouldn't quit their jobs and move into the woods to get away from the world, although it's a great idea, but they do have to stop putting an importance on the things of the world. A job is just a job. It's not going to get you to Heaven, it's going to pay your bills. And how common is it to have a job one day, and then the next it's gone?

"If we were content with the bare minimum like Jesus had, we would be at peace knowing that God would provide it for us if we're faithful to Him. But we all know the bare minimum isn't good enough for us, we want more and better. So, we spend our lives working for the world and not God to feed our vanities.

"Remember, Jesus is God! He could have had anything he wanted—a palace, servants, etc.—but no, He chose to live in poverty, with the bare minimum of possessions. I guess, we're more entitled than Jesus was. Imagine going before God, having given the bare minimum of your time to Him, and expecting to be saved from the damnation of Hell. It doesn't make any sense.

"If you live your life for the world, you can be assured that Jesus is not going to be standing there with open arms welcoming you at the moment of death. It doesn't work that way. Put yourself in Jesus's position. If you knew somebody and loved them deeply but they spent their whole life paying little or no attention to you, would you welcome them with open arms? Of course not. You'd say, 'I'm sorry, but I barely know you.' That's exactly what happens when we die and have lived a life for the world.

"People are completely oblivious to any of this information because it goes against what the world tells you is necessary of your life: 'just be a good person and you'll waltz your way into Heaven.' *Wrong!* God has made it very clear to us that living the life of a good person is not nearly enough to be saved, and do you know what happens when I tell people this? They get angry and bad-mouth me. This ridiculous life here on Earth is so important to them that they can't conceive living it any other way than what they're used to. People are so desperate for these petty little seventy or eighty years we have here on Earth to be as pleasant as possible. They work so hard to secure a comfortable environment for themselves that they completely ignore their eternity. *Eternity!* Think about that. Billions and billions of years will go by and if you're in Hell you'll be suffering forever. You'll have nothing but regret for your spiritual laziness and lack of preparation for the next world. And one more thing, you'll have nobody to blame but yourself.

"I've actually heard people say 'Oh well, I guess I'll end up in hell,' and they say it like Hell isn't so bad. Think of the greatest sufferings you can encounter on earth, whether it's a disease or any other horrific scenario you can think of, any of this would be like a delightful day at the beach compared to one minute in Hell.

"I've also heard people say 'I'll see all my friends there. We'll all be together.' They don't understand that Hell is a place of hatred. You may see your very best friend there, but you will hate them. You'll hate them with a hatred you've never known before. Hell is not a place where you're going to sit down and have a beer with your buddy, you'll be blaming each other for being there. You'll feel it's his fault, and he'll feel the same. All those things that you did together, which were offending God, will be the ammunition which you'll blame each other for. You'll have such hatred for each other and everybody else around you and it'll last forever—constant fighting and blasphemies for all time. If you think you're having a hard time now, wait until you're in Hell, except that will never end.

"We know exactly what Hell is like from the mystics and visionaries of the church. It's no mystery, just read about Padre Pio's visions of hell if you want to have a better understanding of it, and that's just one of many examples. If people would just take the time to learn about their faith, they could prepare themselves. How foolish and lazy we are. What are you going to do in Hell, think back to the big beautiful house you lived in? That awesome car you just had to have? All the great vacations you took and all that great sex you had? Yeah, that's worth an eternity in Hell, I'm sure. People live for now, for this stupid world that does nothing but disappoint. They're living to serve the devil and don't even know it. If people don't open their eyes and make some serious changes, they'll be lost forever. And again, they will have nobody to blame but themselves. Live with that for eternity."

Chapter 9

Understanding Sin

"One thing I don't understand, Father, is the few number of people I see going to confession each week. It seems that we're constantly offending God, yet nobody's confessing these sins."

"You have no idea the indifference that goes on with confession. It all boils down to people not understanding sin. I've been hearing confessions for nearly forty years, and the most common thing I hear is 'I can't really think of anything I've done wrong.' There're people who haven't gone to confession for years, and I mean, decades! Yet they come into confession and that's what they say. People are their own worst enemy.

They know so little about their faith that they can't even recognize their own sins.

"We all sin, and God is gracious enough to grant us forgiveness for these sins. Without it, we would all end up in Hell without exception. Of course, God's love for us is so great that He's thought of that. So, we have this wonderful gift of forgiveness and people aren't using it. Going to confession and not confessing anything because you don't think you've sinned doesn't release you from those sins. Confessing them with true repentance and making reparation through penance releases you from these sins.

"I get another one in confession from certain people, too. 'I'm sorry for anything I may have done to offend God.' Nothing specific is confessed here, just a generalization of sin. 'What I may have done,' that's what you're confessing? I hate to disappoint you but it doesn't work like that. Your specific sins must be confessed. Once again, people have their own ideas about how things work with God and they swear they're right! Even people who consider themselves learned about the faith do this kind of stuff. They're so ignorant and they don't even know it."

"What would you say are the most common sins we commit?" I ask Father.

"Well, the most commonly confessed sins are sins of the flesh—sex. Many people who shouldn't be having sex because they're not married in the church are having sex on a regular basis. They're not married properly in the church for a variety of reasons, but they rationalize to themselves that it's okay and how they're living isn't their fault or sinful. It's the church's or someone else's fault that they're not married properly. They'll convince themselves of this, and live their lives according to their ways of understanding. Many times, it's due to divorce. But remember that Jesus said, 'What therefore God has joined together, let not man put asunder' (Matthew 10:9). This means that divorce is forbidden. Now I know that marriages can go bad and often the person you married ends up being someone completely different, but that doesn't give you permission to divorce that person and start over with someone new. If you do divorce, then you're choosing to spend the rest of your life without a mate. I know many will say that that's unfair, but that's what God has said. However, if you do divorce and end up in a relationship with someone, you'd better be celibate, because no matter how you try to justify it to yourself, it is a serious mortal sin. You see, we pick and choose the rules we decide to follow in this life. If it opposes our will, it doesn't apply to us. So, you make a concise decision to disobey one of Gods laws and do your own will, but God will be there welcoming you at the moment of death? Good luck with that logic. Now if your spouse dies, you're free to remarry. The Church has always taught that.

"Of course, today, sex is just a part of everyday life. There's no thought of marriage first anymore. Everyone's having sex outside of marriage. Even young people are having sex today. It's just accepted. Schools and parents even encourage it by teaching safe sex, by teaching the use of various contraception. Shouldn't the teachings be not having sex? Parents don't understand that it is their responsibility to educate and discourage sex outside of marriage. Whether you child is in their teens, twenties, thirties, etc. it's your responsibility to do everything you can to prevent these instances, and if you fail to do everything within your power, you may bear the burden of sin for their actions. By turning a blind eye, you are essentially giving consent. Remember you're their parent, not their friend, always keep their best interest at heart. Self-denial is a thing of the past, just do what makes you happy. It'll be alright.

"How about those who point their finger at homosexuals who are having sex? News flash! If you're not married properly in the church, your heterosexual sex is just as offensive to God as homosexual sex. Again, people make up the rules as it applies best to their lives. Whatever they can do to convince themselves that how they're living is okay will suit them just fine. But you can be assured that God has a different understanding of things, and He's not going to sit there at your particular judgment and listen to the rationalization of your choices.

"Now, you might think that because you're married properly in the church that it's always okay to have sex with your spouse."

"Isn't it?" I ask.

"Certainly not. You can easily commit the sin of lust with your spouse. There's a big difference between *making love* and *having sex*. If you're making love, it's an expression of your feelings for that person. It's tenderness, love, affection, respect, care, etc. You're sharing a wonderful gift that God has bestowed on the two of you. But how easy is it to have sex just because you have the desire to have sex? There are very few truly happy marriages. I'm convinced of that because I've been counseling and hearing the problems of married couples for a long time. Without exaggeration, I can count on one hand the amount of happy and successful marriages I've seen. Now, just because you're still together and not divorced doesn't mean that your marriage is successful. Many couples spend much of their time arguing over everything. This goes on practically daily. Do you really think that these people, who can barely be in the same room with each other without arguing, are expressing their love for each other when they decide it's time for sex, or are they just satisfying their physical needs? It's not love, you can be assured of that. This would be committing the very serious sin of lust.

"Other very common sins are sins of anger. People are always so angry with everyone around them. We seem to have a very difficult time forgiving people. Let's say someone offends you by either their words or actions. Sometimes, even after an apology is given, we're still angry and offended by them. This is incredible pride. First, who are you that you shouldn't be offended by someone? Have you forgotten that you've offended God countless times? And every time you went to God to ask forgiveness for that offense, didn't He forgive you immediately? So, who are you that you're so important that your toes shouldn't be stepped on? How dare you have such arrogance about yourself? Perhaps you're so perfect that you've never offended anybody before. People should take a good honest look at themselves in the mirror.

"Now, if you're so unwilling to give forgiveness to someone who's offended you, why should God extend you the same courtesy? Maybe the rules don't apply to you. The truth is, we think we're so important that we're above being offended by another. Do people ever consider that God may have allowed you to be offended so you can have the opportunity to practice patience, humility, and forgiveness? I'll explain it more simply: *it's a test!* God is constantly testing us to prepare us for things to come. We are so willing to hold a grudge against someone for the smallest offense. These grudges can go on for years. What do you gain from that? All it does is rob you of your peace, and it allows that person to control you.

"Imagine dying suddenly while having anger or even hatred in your heart for someone or for something that may even be rather insignificant that they did to you. Now you're going to ask and expect forgiveness from God for your offenses, don't you think God might say 'You were unwilling to forgive that person, so why would I forgive you?'

"'Unless you change and become as little children, you will not enter the kingdom of Heaven' (Matthew 18:3). Think about that statement. How different are children from adults with their approach to the world? It partly means to put your pride away and be willing to accept being offended by others. When a child gets mad over something, it doesn't last long at all. A few minutes later, they're back to their old self. They've moved past and forgotten about it. We must take the same approach to these instances when somebody walks all over us. Jesus says it: 'You will not enter the kingdom of Heaven.' What more needs to be explained? He's telling us what to do! We'd better get over ourselves pretty quickly and stop thinking we're so important, or we'll pay for it with our souls.

"We have a big problem in this world with sin—understanding, acknowledging, and making reparation for them. People need to start educating themselves on their faith or they're going to be lost. I don't really know how people can have such a lack of knowledge about sin. Things are so accepted today, even within the church, that people are completely ignorant of committing sin. We offend God every day, yet people think that as long as they're not Hitler, they're doing alright. Criminals, thieves, drug dealers, terrorists, gang members—those are the people who offend God. I'm okay. God's perfectly happy and satisfied with me. How incredibly foolish our thinking can be.

"Anger, jealousy, impatience, laziness— just a few things we do all the time that offend God. Nobody is guilty of these and a hundred other offenses like them? Some of the greatest sins we can commit are sins of neglect, things we don't do, and when we replace our spiritual life with the world. Take spiritual reading. We're all obliged to do spiritual reading, and why? Because our purpose here on earth is to know, love, and serve God. Well, if you don't learn about Him, how can you know Him? And if you don't know Him, how can you love Him? And if you don't love Him, why would you serve Him? But how lazy are we to pick up a spiritual book? Instead, the TV goes on. This is spiritual laziness, and it is incredibly offensive to God.

"How many people actually read, study, and think about the Ten Commandments or the seven deadly sins? You'd be surprised how many of these sins we are committing daily. There're two people who've lived on earth who were sinless—Jesus and the Blessed Mother. That's it! Amazing how people think they're on the same level as Jesus and His Mother.

"How many people say they're going to pray but find something more interesting on TV instead? Or revolve their prayers around their TV schedule? The things we allow to distract us from God are everywhere. We need to shut out these simple pleasures we allow ourselves and put God first. 'Pray unceasingly.' Direct words from Jesus Himself. He didn't say, 'Pray and then put on your favorite TV program.' 'Pray without ceasing' (Thessalonians 5:17). That means every opportunity you have should be spent with God. When you're working, you should center that work on

God, and when you're not working, find something to do that will draw you closer to God, whether it's through prayer, spiritual reading, or maybe watching a good movie or documentary about Jesus or some saint. There's a lot of ways to keep yourself close to God, but going out into the world will only draw you into sin. The world is a distraction to your spiritual life! You may not even realize that you're sinning because it can be very innocent what you're doing, but is it worth the risk to your soul? When we've done all we're supposed to do to draw ourselves to God daily, then we can enjoy some free time to relax a bit. Use that time as you see fit. But we must fulfill our obligations to God first and it's a lot more than going to church once a week, I can promise you that.

"Always remember that the devil is constantly by us, urging us to sin and for forgetfulness of God. It should be our highest priority to make God a constant presence in our daily lives. If we don't, we will forget about Him, and the sins will continue to mount up. By doing this, we're storing tremendous fuel for the fires of purgatory, or even worse, Hell. 'You know not the day nor the hour' (Matthew 25:13). At any time, Jesus can come and say to you, 'This very day, your soul is required of you.' Everyone should take a very serious and honest look at themselves and ask the question, 'Am I prepared to meet God in judgment today?'"

Chapter 10

The Fewness of the Saved

"You said something before, Father, that kind of bothered me: 'The fewness of the saved.' What's that all about?"

"That's something nobody wants to hear about, and I tell you that from much experience. Some of the greatest saints of the church have taught this very thing and it's as scary as it gets. This teaching is so disturbing that most people refuse to even acknowledge it, but it's a very important teaching, and if understood by people, they would have no choice but to alter their lives, yet I've found that this is where people draw the line. They absolutely refuse to believe it, to accept it as church teachings, or even consider it to apply to them. It's the reason why you hear at funerals these days: 'They're in a better place now.' This is ignorance at its greatest levels. I've already explained it—nobody goes directly to Heaven. Get it out of your head because it just isn't so. This thought is so terrifying to most people that they pretend it doesn't exist. I hate to burst your spiritual bubbles, but ignoring it doesn't make it go away.

"I get so confused by people. They plan so diligently for every aspect of their human lives, always preparing for the next step. But for eternity, nobody makes any effort at all. As a matter of fact, it's basically ignored. How can people do that? How can you work so hard and plan so rigorously for a future that is so uncertain, for something you may not even be alive for? You might not be here tomorrow, shouldn't your main efforts go toward the thing you will definitely experience? Your afterlife! This kind of thing dumbfounds me.

"There's a long list of saints who have preached the fewness of the saved. I've given sermons on it and have tried to teach people about it. But wow! How people react to me when I bring it up. Great saints such as St. Leonard of Port Maurice, St. Theodore, St. Basil, St. John Chrysostom, and St. Simeon Stylites have all taught the very few number of people who are saved due to their lack of love for God and their attachment to the love of the world.

"I think most people would actually be bored in Heaven. Not only that, but if you told them that when they die they are going to go directly to Heaven to spend their eternity with Jesus, they would be puzzled. Why would anyone want to spend their eternity with someone they don't know or have any interest in? It seems like that would be their Hell! If you have no interest in something, you certainly don't spend any of your time indulging in that particular thing. It's the same thing when it comes to God and Heaven. If your interests don't lie with God now, it's certainly not going to magically change when you die.

"Love for God is what gets us into Heaven. It's that simple. A person can try to rationalize their life any way they want, to make themselves feel better now, but that will end with death. People lie to themselves because they're so afraid to face reality. When someone dies, it's hard to imagine that person isn't in Heaven. We try to convince ourselves of this because we want to relate these beliefs to our own lives. Nobody, including myself, wants to think about going to Hell. It's a scary thought. But understanding how to be saved, not ignoring it, and not lying to ourselves to the point that we believe ourselves will get us to Heaven. It would be like finding out that you have a deadly disease, and instead of acknowledging it, seeking help, and dealing with it, you ignore it in the hopes that it just won't be a reality. Now if you did that, you would certainly die from that untreated illness. The same principle applies to your soul. If you ignore it, it will die and suffer for all eternity. You would think that the possibility of going to Hell would get people to do everything in their power to change their lives, but since most don't think that Hell is a possibility for them, they make no efforts at all.

"When you have people who could perform miracles, who bore the stigmata, people who lived their lives in ways that we can't even comprehend like St. Simeon Stylites, who lived thirty-seven years on top of a pillar for love of God, tell us about the fewness of the saved, we should probably listen to them. It's not some nut standing on a street corner yelling about his own opinion. These are people chosen by God to relate these truths to us. Unfortunately, we place such importance in our own opinions that these warnings fall on deaf ears.

"When you think of how little people do in preparation for their next life, it makes perfect sense. People are damning themselves because of their indifferentism to God. It's the love of this world and the attachment to material possessions that will be most people's demise."

"I would think that people should be working tirelessly to understand and avoid sin at all cost, knowing how deadly it can be to your soul," I say.

"Logic would make you think that, but I can assure you that's not the case. Either people don't care or they just can't believe that it's so. People are happy with the way they live their lives, they don't want anything disrupting it. That's why people accept the modernism of the church today. It allows you to do what you want. Not what God wants. The church has changed so drastically over the past fifty years, do you really think God is pleased with so many of His teachings just being tossed away so we can do what makes us happy? You'd have to be a fool to believe that. Today, it's all about what makes for a happy life here on earth— the exact opposite of what Christ taught.

"People may not accept the teaching of the fewness of the saved in this life, but I can assure you that it will be understood and accepted at the moment of death. And oh how people will regret how they gave their life to the world."

Chapter 11

Conquering Death

"There's so much more to death than people realize. We're under this impression that when we die we're going to go through some tunnellike thing with a bright light at the end, and when we get through it, we'll be in Heaven. This couldn't be any further from what really happens when we die."

"Okay, what are we in store for?" I ask.

"Well, we know from the teachings of Jesus and the many mystics and visionaries who've had interactions with God and had many visions of death, Heaven, Hell, and so on that we're in for a tremendous spiritual battle when we die."

"A battle? What do you mean by a spiritual battle?" I anxiously ask.

"This is something that practically nobody knows about and most people will refuse to accept. When we die, not only do we go before God in judgment, but we will, and I say will because it *will* happen to each and every one of us, be assailed by the devil. Now I know you're going to ask what that means, so let me explain it.

"When our Lord went through His agony in the garden, He was assailed by the devil who reproached Him with imaginary crimes. The devil tried to get Jesus to accept responsibility for certain things that happened, such as the Massacre of the Innocents, the beheading of John the Baptist, and many more things as sins and crimes that He was responsible for. The devil is a master of deceit, and he knows exactly how to make your mind waver. So at the hour of your death, you will be approached by Satan himself, and God allows this. Satan will try his hardest to exaggerate and distort all the sins of your life to get you to commit the only sin that is unforgivable by

God. He will try to have you commit the sin of despair. The sin of despair is thinking that your sins are greater than God's mercy. There is nothing that is greater than Gods' love, forgiveness, and mercy for us. But since Satan is the ultimate master if deceit, he can convince you that your sins are simply too horrific to be forgiven by God. It will be at that moment that you may give up your faith and trust in God and fall into despair. Now, you're going to appear before God thinking that all He did for us by dying the most ignominious death was all in vain, therefore we end up damning ourselves to Hell. It is a direct insult to the love God has for us—to think that the faults and weaknesses we had during this life that caused us to sin is greater than what God went through for us on the cross. It is the ultimate sin of despair, and it is the only sin we cannot be forgiven for. Judas is a fitting example of this. Judas betraying Jesus seems to be the ultimate sin ever committed by anyone, yet if Judas had gone to Jesus and admitted his betrayal and repented of it, he would have been forgiven instantly by Jesus and gone to heaven, but since he felt his sin was to great, he fell into despair and hung himself. We know now that Judas sits at the right hand of Satan himself, in hell, for all eternity.

"Many people who were in a state of grace and who could have gone to Heaven are now in Hell for all eternity because, at their last moments, they lost their faith in God's love and mercy for them. You might understand now how important it is to receive Holy Communion daily. By receiving communion daily, you'll build a bond between yourself and Christ. This personal bond of love between the two of you may be the very thing that saves your soul from damnation.

"It's the same with having a devotion to the saints. If you find a saint that you can relate, connect with, and pray to, they will be there at the hour of your death to help fight off this assault from the devil. Do you see how spending all your time being involved in the world and giving nothing extra to God will end up damning your soul? How can you develop the spiritual weapons you'll need to survive this assault that will happen to every one of us by only going to church once a week?

"People have no idea what they're in store for when they die. It's the sad reality of today's world. This kind of thing used to be regular church teachings, but now the church has left its people completely unprepared for their death. When you go to a funeral today, the priest says 'Aunt Millie is now in Heaven with Jesus.' They don't even acknowledge purgatory anymore! It's been completely eliminated. Nobody even has any sins that need to be purged. Everybody goes directly to Heaven. So now that soul that may be in purgatory is left completely abandoned. Souls in purgatory can do nothing to help themselves. They are left totally reliant on the prayers of us here on earth. Now if a soul is in Heaven, why would you pray for them? They're in Heaven, they don't need any prayers. Everything is perfect for them. But if they're in purgatory, they're suffering more than you can possibly comprehend. And the only thing that can bring them relief at that point is people praying for them. But this absurd belief that you're in Heaven automatically leaves these poor souls suffering alone without prayers because we've been told that that soul is already in Heaven. It is literally an evil being taught by the church today, and they should be ashamed of themselves.

"Everything that Christ taught us has been completely dumbed down. When Pope John XXIII said he was going to 'adjust the church to the world,' he sure did a good job. And in its wake, he's left many people paying for it with their eternal soul."

Chapter 12

The Point Is . . .

"Wow! That's a lot of scary stuff to think about, Father."

"It sure is. And if people actually thought about it, they might get somewhere with their spiritual journey. Unfortunately, it requires several things like being honest with yourself and do something that many people are uncomfortable with, and that's thinking about and acknowledging your own death. Many people are simply too scared to sit down and think about death. It's just too much for them. The bad part is that you're not preparing for your death. You will die! It's going to happen, and trying to pretend that it's not a part of your future will not make it go away.

"There's been a terrible breakdown of reality in the church today. To go to the Catholic Church today and be told that you're assured of Heaven when you die is without a doubt going to put you in Hell. Of course, nobody would admit it. They would all say I'm crazy and that I don't know what I'm talking about. But I know church teachings and what I'm telling you is fact.

"The difference between a good person and a so-called bad person is that the bad person simply acknowledges the fact that they make mistakes and sin, they do things like go to confession, and try to make improvements in their spiritual life. They're not under the impression that because they live a moral life, they're without sin. They recognize their weaknesses and faults. They seek God to try to strengthen and improve themselves to draw themselves closer to God. That's what good people going to hell and bad people going to Heaven is all about.

"'I say to you, that even so there shall be joy in Heaven upon one sinner that does penance, more than upon ninety-nine just who need not penance' (Luke 15:7). If you believe that you don't sin and you don't need to go before God and confess your sins and do penance on a regular basis, boy, are you going to be in for a big surprise when you die. The church today obliges you to go to confession once a year during Lent. Once a year! You're willing to carry around sins on your soul for a full year! That's a very dangerous game to play.

"When I was a kid, and the church taught regularly the seriousness of sin, and how often we commit them, (unfortunately something not taught anymore); the church would be packed every Saturday with people going to confession; there would be five or six priests there all day hearing them, because people were aware of how important it is to understand and acknowledge their sins before God regularly, because of course, we know that we can die at any given moment. What the church has done to people today in not teaching them the truths about death is shameful. People are gambling with their eternal soul. When you die, that's it. There won't be another chance.

"People need to wake up and start taking God seriously. If we're here to serve God, perhaps you should ask yourself exactly how you do that every day. I bet most people wouldn't have an answer for themselves. We've become very comfortable with ourselves and the embracement of the world, but it's this world that will lead to your damnation, whether you believe it or not. How I pray every day that our hearts and minds will open to the reality of what's expected of us from God and to earn that eternal glory. God provides everything we need to understand what we must do for salvation. They're called graces, and God provides enough of them for all of us. As difficult as it may be, you must turn your back on the world. We must deny ourselves our little creature comforts and sacrifice ourselves for the love of God. Don't risk your soul's eternal salvation because you were so in love with the world. Trust me, God loves you more than the world ever could."

"Father, this is really important information that people should hear about? I know you preach this kind of stuff all the time, but how about the people who aren't here and never hear these things?"

"The problem is that if the average person heard what I'm telling you, they would probably reject it! They don't want to hear this kind of information. People don't take change well, especially change to their beliefs about something. This stuff is on a completely different level than where the average person is at. They don't know these things, and they don't want to know them. People decide what's right for their lives based on what they want. Nobody, including God, can tell them differently. I've had conversations with people about these very subjects and they've gotten so angry with me. I've even had people simply get up and walk away. People don't want to think of anything unpleasant. They're happy in their perfect little worlds. They've convinced themselves that everything is fine and that they and everyone they know will die and go directly to Heaven, and they're perfectly satisfied with that. You've heard the old saying, 'Ignorance is bliss.' This is very true."

"Well, I think this is important information and people need to hear it," I say.

"They sure do. But how do you get people to listen? Not only that, how do you get a person to change their way of thinking? A change is required to live a life serving God. Living a life for God and not the world isn't comfortable at all. It's hard and tiring. It's the narrow and thorny path, but it's the only path that leads to Heaven. Most people have forgotten that."

"You're right Father, people have forgotten that. But what if there was a way for us to bring these teachings to people's attention? Wouldn't that perhaps get people to do some thinking? And possibly begin making some changes in the way they view their eternal destiny? I don't know about you but I think whatever we could do would be worth it. Have you ever considered writing a book?"

"Write a book! What do we know about writing a book? Have you ever written anything before?"

"No, I haven't. But maybe that's something God would want from us," I respond.

"Well, if we don't know anything about it, how can we write a book? I wouldn't even know where to begin," Father says.

"I don't know," I respond. "We may not know anything about it, but if God wants us to, we can write a book."

Examination of Conscience

God has given us the Ten Commandments as a way to guide us through life and help us to avoid sinning as much as possible. The Seven Deadly Sins are excellent examples of sin, and how we can fall into committing them. This examination of conscience will help explain how we can be guilty of committing each one. Consider them as a preparation for confession.

The Ten Commandments

First Commandment: I am the Lord thy God, thou shall not have strange gods before me.

• Missing Mass on Sunday,

- Unnecessary or manual work on Sunday, and
- Worldly pursuits before spiritual growth (mental prayer, spiritual reading).
- Worshiping any creature or thing, by giving honor and perfection that belongs to God alone

Second Commandment: Thou shall not take the name of the Lord thy God in vain.

- Curse to call down evil on a person, place, or thing,
- I blasphemed the name of Jesus and/or Christ,
- I cursed others by saying "God damn you,"
- I cursed my spouse or children,
- I cursed in the hearing of the young,
- I perjured myself by swearing falsely in court,
- I took rash and unnecessary oaths,
- I provoked others to curse,
- I did not prevent cursing when I could and should have, and

- I spoke against saints, holy things, and pious practices.

Third Commandment: Remember to keep Holy the Sabbath Day.

- I missed Mass on Sunday and Holy Days of Obligation through my own fault,
- I spent part of the day in sinful occupations,
- I was late for Mass unjustly,
- I kept my wife or children from Mass,
- I assisted at Mass with willful distractions, and
- I engaged in manual labor on Sundays and Holy Days without necessity.

Fourth Commandment: Honor thy father and mother.
(Duty of Children)

- I disobeyed my parents,
- I caused them to be angry,

- I used insulting language,
- I did not support them,
- I incited my brothers and sisters against them, and
- I neglected them in sickness and death.

(Duty of Husbands and Fathers)

- I grieved, abused, and/or struck my wife,
- I accused her wrongly,
- I neglected to provide for my family,
- I gave my children bad example,
- I failed to correct their faults, and
- I neglected to instruct them in religion.

(Duties of Wives and Mothers)

- I disobeyed my husband,
- I caused my children to disobey and dishonor him,
- I talked of his faults to my children or neighbors,

- I neglected to correct my children,
- I gave them bad example,
- I did not instruct them in religion, and
- I interfered with their religious vocation.

Fifth Commandment: Thou shall not kill.

- I was unjustly angry,
- I caused others to be unjustly angry,
- I was unjustly quarreling or fighting,
- I desired the death of others,
- I cherished hatred to others,
- I refused to speak or to be reconciled to others,
- I caused the death of another by negligence,
- I led others to commit sin, by word or example, and
- Caused, counseled, and/or consented to abortion.

Sixth Commandment: Though shalt not commit adultery.

- Fornication outside of marriage,
- Lusting for another,
- Causing others to lust, and
- Immodest dress.

Seventh Commandment: Thou shalt not steal.

- Taking things that do not belong to you,
- Getting paid for work not performed,
- Not paying for work performed, and
- I neglected to pay my bills and just debts.

Eighth Commandment: Thou shalt not bear false witness against thy neighbor.

- I told lies,
- I destroyed my neighbor's reputation,

- I gossiped about my neighbor, and
- I failed to make reparation for sins of the tongue.

Ninth Commandment: Thou shalt not covet thy neighbor's wife.

- Desire wrongly my neighbor's wife, and
- Trying to seduce my neighbor's wife.

Tenth Commandment: Thou shalt not covet thy neighbor's goods.

- Desire wrongly my neighbor's possessions, and
- Trying to acquire my neighbor's possessions.

The Seven Deadly Sins

Pride:

- My will be done, not yours,
- Falling in love with ourselves (boasting of physical stature, intelligence, abilities), and
- Feeling superiority toward others.

Covetousness:

- Desiring wrongly someone else's good fortune, and
- Resenting someone else's talents and abilities.

Lust:

- Complete opposite of love, and

- Your attraction lies only in the physical.

Anger:

- Acting on your emotions of anger.

Gluttony:

- Lack of control over your appetites (food, drink, drugs).

Envy:

- Jealousy of others (possessions, beauty, intelligence, talents).

Sloth:

- Laziness (parents not teaching their children discipline, not doing your job to your employers' expectations, those in a position of authority not correcting problems when they arise).

About the Author

Jay and Fr. Bernard

Father Bernard Champagne began his religious experience, when at the age of three, his mother started taking him to daily Mass. Growing up in Haverhill Massachusetts, he attended Catholic school from the first grade through high school. During his teenage years, he would write short religious articles that were printed in the local papers. After high school, he joined the Trappist religious order where he became a monk. He spent the next twenty years cloistered from the world in a monastery in Spencer Massachusetts and living the monastic life in a Benedictine monastery. Those years were spent in the daily education of Catholicism

Christianity and all of its aspects, as well as voluntarily learning about most other religions. He eventually chose to serve God by becoming a priest. Now, in his eighties, his thirst for knowledge and the understanding of religion has never diminished, and he continues to expand his vast expertise.

Jay McCurtten is a student of Catholicism, Christianity, and Protestantism. Being mentored by Fr. Bernard, he juggles his time between work, family, and daily religious studies. In addition, he also acts as a Mass lector and altar server at Fr. Bernard's church. Being ever grateful for having the opportunity to acquire such life changing information, he vowed to find a way to pass these teachings onto others. Being a first-time author, it was a wonderful serendipity to discover the ability to communicate, in an interesting and effective way, the written word. His daily studies continue, and his authorship is just beginning.

CPSIA information can be obtained
at www.ICGtesting.com
Printed in the USA
BVHW07s1454040618
518159BV00001B/30/P

9 781641 386456